STECK-VAUGHN
PORTRAIT OF AMERICA

Pennsylvania

Steck-Vaughn Company
      Executive Editor   Diane Sharpe
      Senior Editor   Martin S. Saiewitz
      Design Manager   Pamela Heaney
      Photo Editor   Margie Foster

Proof Positive/Farrowlyne Associates, Inc.
Program Editorial, Revision Development, Design, and Production

Consultant: Robert A. McNary, Director of Marketing, Pennsylvania Department of Commerce

Published by Raintree Steck-Vaughn Publishers, an imprint of Steck-Vaughn Company.

A Turner Educational Services, Inc. book. Based on the Portrait of America television series by R. E. (Ted) Turner.

Cover Photo: Barn by © Superstock.

Library of Congress Cataloging-in-Publication Data

Thompson, Kathleen.
      Pennsylvania / Kathleen Thompson.
            p.   cm. — (Portrait of America)
      "Based on the Portrait of America television series"—T.p. verso.
      "A Turner book."
      Includes index.
      ISBN 0-8114-7383-X (library binding).—ISBN 0-8114-7464-X (softcover)
      1. Pennsylvania—Juvenile literature. I. Title. II. Series:
Thompson, Kathleen. Portrait of America.
F149.3.T46   1996
974.8—dc20   95-9609
                                                                                        CIP
                                                                                        AC

Printed and Bound in the United States of America

3 4 5 6 7 8 9 10 WZ 03 02 01

Acknowledgments
The publishers wish to thank the following for permission to reproduce photographs:
P. 7 National Park Service; p. 8 North Wind Picture Archives; p. 11 The Free Library of Philadelphia; p. 12 Pennsylvania Office of Travel Marketing; p. 13 The Free Library of Philadelphia; p. 14 (top) The Free Library of Philadelphia, (bottom) Philadelphia Convention and Visitors Bureau; p. 15 Philadelphia Convention and Visitors Bureau; p. 16 (top) Pennsylvania Office of Travel Marketing, (bottom) Photograph from the collection of the Pennsylvania Historical & Museum Commission's Drake Well Museum in Titusville, PA.; p. 17 (top) The Carnegie Library of Pittsburgh, (bottom) North Wind Picture Archives; p. 18 Historical Collections and Labor Archives, Penn State; p. 19 Wisconsin Historical Society; p. 20 The Bettmann Archive; p. 21 GPU Nuclear Corporation; p. 22 Philadelphia Convention and Visitors Bureau; p. 23 The Historical Society of Pennsylvania; p. 24 The Library of Congress; p. 25 Historical Collections and Labor Archives, Penn State; p. 26 Bethlehem Steel; p. 28 The Woolworth Corporation; p. 29 (top) PA Dutch Convention & Visitors Bureau, (bottom) Bethlehem Steel; pp. 30 & 31 © Grant Heilman Photography; pp. 32 & 33 Photos courtesy Hershey Foods Corporation; p. 34 © Grant Heilman Photography; p. 36 The Bettmann Archive; p. 37 AP/Wide World; pp. 38 & 39 The Bettmann Archive; p. 40 © Andrew Wagner/The Greater Pittsburgh Convention and Visitors Bureau; p. 42 (top) The Library of Congress, (bottom) PA Dutch Convention & Visitors Bureau; p. 43 © Herb Moskovitz/Mummers Museum; p. 44 Philadelphia Convention and Visitors Bureau; p. 46 One Mile Up; p. 47 (left) One Mile Up, (center & right) Pennsylvania Office of Travel Marketing.

STECK-VAUGHN

PORTRAIT OF AMERICA

Pennsylvania

Kathleen Thompson

A Turner Book

RSVP

RAINTREE
STECK-VAUGHN
PUBLISHERS
The Steck-Vaughn Company

Austin, Texas

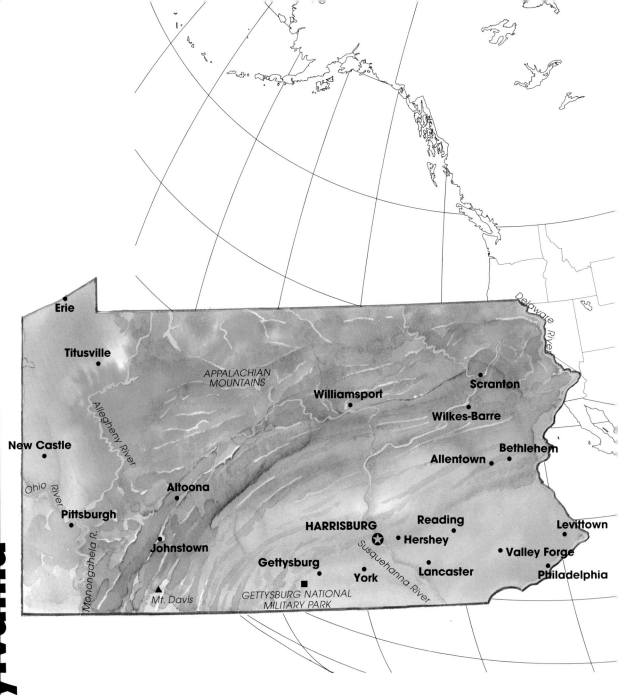

Pennsylvania

Erie

Titusville

APPALACHIAN
MOUNTAINS

Williamsport

Scranton

Wilkes-Barre

New Castle

Allegheny River

Bethlehem

Allentown

Ohio River

Altoona

Pittsburgh

Monongahela R.

Johnstown

HARRISBURG

Reading

Hershey

Levittown

Susquehanna River

Valley Forge

Gettysburg

Lancaster

Philadelphia

York

Mt. Davis

GETTYSBURG NATIONAL
MILITARY PARK

Delaware River

Contents

Introduction

Many things that we call American began in Pennsylvania. Freedom of religion inspired William Penn to found the colony that was named for him. Benjamin Franklin thought that a community should create institutions to serve all its citizens. So he organized in Pennsylvania some things we take for granted today: a fire department, a public library, and an insurance company. Then, the best and brightest people of the day gathered in Pennsylvania. They wrote the documents that created our nation—the Declaration of Independence and the United States Constitution.

Today, the same spirit of tolerance, community, and creativity is alive and well in Pennsylvania. It gives the state its vital character. It forms the keystone of Pennsylvania today.

Philadelphia's Independence Hall was the site of some of the most important events in early American history.

Pennsylvania

Quakers, steel, coal, immigrants, robber barons

"Virtue, Liberty, and Independence"

Pennsylvania's history goes back much further than its motto, "Virtue, Liberty, and Independence." Before Columbus landed on this continent, a group of Native Americans called the Lenni-Lenape hunted and farmed in the Delaware River Basin. The Susquehannock were living along the banks of the Susquehanna River, in the southeastern part of what would soon be called Pennsylvania.

Both the Lenni-Lenape and the Susquehannock were farmers, for the most part. They lived and farmed in villages and only sometimes fished or hunted for extra food. Many Europeans thought, however, that the Susquehannock were more warlike than the Lenni-Lenape, probably because of their defensive battles with the aggressive Iroquois people. Their towns were _palisaded_—which means surrounded by tall, pointed stakes—to protect themselves against the Iroquois. But their palisades would not be enough to protect them against either the Iroquois or European settlement.

Philadelphians removed the British king's coat of arms from above a door in Independence Hall shortly after the United States declared its independence in 1776.

The first Europeans to settle in this area were Swedes. They traveled north from Delaware and founded a colony they called New Sweden in 1643. They were governed by Johan Printz, who made Tinicum Island his capital. For the next several years, other Europeans came into the area and established trading posts. Most of these traders were Dutch. Soon the Swedish settlers and the Dutch began fighting. Then in 1655 Peter Stuyvesant, the governor of New Netherland, took control of New Sweden. Stuyvesant governed until 1664, when the English took the whole region in the name of the Duke of York.

In 1681 King Charles II awarded William Penn a charter making him the owner of a vast area of land. The land was called Pennsylvania, which means Penn's woodland. The name was accurate. "Penn's woodland" was a rich land of woods and rivers.

William Penn was a Quaker. The Quakers were a new religious group in England. They were Christian but had stricter rules on keeping peace and bestowing generosity, among other things. The Quakers had often run into religious persecution in Europe. Penn decided that his new Quaker colony would provide freedom for all other religions, too.

By this time, many colonists had come to the new land to find a place where they could worship as they pleased. But most of the colonies they founded did not have religious freedom for any groups other than their own. In the Puritan colonies, for example, you had to be a Puritan and abide by the laws of the church. If you were not a Puritan, you were forced to leave, or worse. Pennsylvania's atmosphere of tolerance for widely varying religious beliefs thus brought settlers from many different places.

In 1682 William Penn came over from England with a state constitution he called the "Frame of Government." He then brought together a general assembly to discuss the government of the new colony. He encouraged fair treatment of the Native Americans who already lived on the land. The assembly then revised the constitution and adopted it in 1683. This second Frame of Government called for a government by the will of the people. The constitution also provided for religious tolerance. It was not changed until 1701, when Penn wrote the "Charter of Privileges." This document gave the people even greater power. It also made the general assembly the colony's only lawmaking body.

William Penn was the founder of Pennsylvania. His hat and clothing are typical of Quaker dress.

For a brief period beginning in 1692, England denied Penn's right to rule the colony, and New York's governor ruled instead. But Penn was restored to his office in 1694, and the colony began a period of growth. The Delaware River Valley provided rich farmland. There were also thousands of acres of white oak trees. This meant lumber for building and for shipping back to Europe. In the early 1700s iron ore was discovered in the area.

Part of the Appalachian Mountain range that extends through Pennsylvania is known as the Pennsylvania Grand Canyon.

With wood and iron, skilled workers among the colonists began the manufacturing that would make Pennsylvania a rich state. Some merchants began to build huge fortunes. And they pushed to have more roads built so that they could trade more easily with the farmers farther inland.

Pennsylvania's early commitment to fair treatment of the Native Americans did not continue as settlers moved farther north and west. Also, part of the land that the English king had given Penn was still claimed by the French. Soon, the French and the Native Americans became allies in a war against the British colonists on much of the East Coast.

The French and Indian War lasted from 1754 to 1763. The Peace of Paris treaty signed on February 10 gave Great Britain title to Canada and all the land east of the Mississippi River. The British soon made treaties with the Native Americans that limited western settlement. But the Pennsylvania colonists, who were unhappy about the treaties, continued to move westward anyway. They also became dissatisfied with British rule.

By 1776 Pennsylvania was one of the largest colonies, with a population of about 300,000. It was also the most advanced colony, largely because of one man—Benjamin Franklin. From about 1730 to 1760, Franklin founded a number of institutions that brought needed services to the people. For example, he published a newspaper called *The Pennsylvania Gazette*. He established a city hospital, and he greatly improved the post office system. He also founded a school known today as the University of Pennsylvania. Franklin also was becoming an important figure in the political activities of the colonies. He helped write the Declaration of Independence, and he even went to France to ask for military and financial help in the struggle against the British.

Pennsylvania earned its nickname, "the Keystone State," during the days leading up to the American Revolution. The name derived from Pennsylvania's

Benjamin Franklin spent so much time reading and writing that he invented bifocal glasses. These have split lenses so that people can both read and see objects far away by using the same pair of glasses.

John Adams, Roger Sherman, Robert R. Livingston, Thomas Jefferson, and Benjamin Franklin stand in front of John Hancock as he signs the Declaration of Independence.

Philadelphia keeps its history alive for visitors. This actor plays the role of Benjamin Franklin.

location near the center of the arch formed by the 13 colonies. Like the keystone—or topmost piece—of an arch, Pennsylvania was an important support in the structure of the government that was coming into being. Pennsylvania—especially Philadelphia—was a military, political, and economic center. Both the First and Second Continental Congresses were held in Philadelphia. The famous Declaration of Independence was signed at the Pennsylvania State House there. The Liberty Bell, which had only been in place for about twenty-five years, was rung for the Declaration's first public reading.

The colonial forces suffered a major defeat at the Battle of Brandywine Creek in September 1777. The colonial troops could not stop the British from capturing Philadelphia. Washington and his troops retreated to Valley Forge during one of the roughest winters of the war. About twenty-five hundred American soldiers died during the winter of 1777-78.

After the war, Philadelphia became the first capital of the new United States government. By the 1780s Philadelphia had a healthy shipbuilding industry and the first Bank of North America. The 1790s brought the first stock exchange and the Insurance Company of North America to the city.

Coal was discovered in Pennsylvania in the late 1700s. This discovery led to a major transportation project. The coal was too heavy to be carried in the wagons that were used for transporting other goods, so Pennsylvania started building canals. Boats on the canals could carry the heavy coal and also iron machinery. Between 1820 and 1840, the "Mainline Project" was built. More than 800 miles of canals and 100 miles of railroads gradually formed the Pennsylvania Canal System. Philadelphia and Pittsburgh were linked by this system in 1834. The project cost millions of dollars and made Pittsburgh a manufacturing center. Just as

These actors portray Revolutionary War soldiers at George Washington's headquarters in Valley Forge.

This cannon was used in the Battle of Gettysburg, July 1863.

The Drake Oil Well near Titusville, built by Edwin Drake in 1859, was the first successful oil well. Unfortunately, Drake failed to patent his methods, and he died in poverty.

this system was being completed, another project began that would make it out of date: the Pennsylvania Railroad, chartered in 1846.

Pennsylvania was leading the nation in other areas as well. In 1859 Edwin Drake drilled the first successful oil well near Titusville. By 1860 Pennsylvania was supplying much of the nation's coal. The coal was used only in northern factories once the Civil War started.

Although Pennsylvania's southern border was along the Mason-Dixon line, there was no doubt that the state belonged to the Union. Philadelphia had a large African American population. Many of the most outspoken abolitionists were from Pennsylvania. Abolitionists wanted to abolish, or end, slavery. Many people in Pennsylvania had been demanding the abolition of slavery. They also wanted to give African Americans their rights as free Americans.

Only one major battle in the Civil War was fought in Pennsylvania, but this battle was the turning point of the war. In 1863 after three days of fighting at Gettysburg, over fifty thousand soldiers lay dead. Casualties were heavy on both sides, but the Union had beaten the forces of Robert E. Lee. The Union had won its first major battle and was on its way to many more victories.

After the war, business boomed again in the state of Pennsylvania. The three big industries were coal, steel, and oil. It was the time of the "robber barons." These were men who made huge fortunes with little care for their underpaid workers. Pennsylvanians Andrew Carnegie, Henry Clay Frick, Joseph and J. Howard Pew, and Andrew W. Mellon became millionaires this way. They created large corporations: Bethlehem Steel, Sun Oil, and United States Steel Corporation, all based in Pennsylvania.

During the late nineteenth century, Andrew Carnegie made millions of dollars manufacturing steel. After he retired, he used some of his vast wealth to establish public libraries all over the world.

The Battle of Gettysburg greatly weakened Confederate forces during the Civil War and marked a turning point in the war in favor of the Union.

Together, these corporations managed to stop the Pennsylvania legislature from passing child labor laws and worker's compensation laws. These companies did not try to improve working conditions or pay more money to their workers. Instead the companies blocked laws that would do that. They also stood in the way of antitrust suits and labor unions that would aid workers.

Working conditions in these companies were often dangerous and unhealthy. Insurance companies would not insure the workers because the risks were too high. Most of the workers in the coal mines and the factories were recent immigrants from Europe and African Americans from the South. These workers began to form organizations that would help provide for each other and their families if they were injured or if they were killed on the job.

Between 1880 and 1936, thousands of coal miners died from illnesses related to working conditions. Children worked in the mines for a few cents a day. Housing conditions for steel workers in Carnegie's

Pennsylvanian iron workers provided some of the raw materials for the steel industry.

steel mills were very bad. When the labor unions tried to organize the workers for better working and living conditions, they were up against not only the companies but the government as well.

A major strike occured in 1902. The dispute was between coal miners in northeastern Pennsylvania and the coal companies. The workers' union, the United Mine Workers, demanded wage increases and an eight-hour workday. When the coal companies refused, one hundred and forty thousand miners walked off the job. The mines closed. With winter coming on, houses, schools, and hospitals were running out of coal. President Theodore Roosevelt established a board of arbitrators to work with both sides.

This young coal-mine worker is holding up a paper showing his wages: 32¢ for 8 hours of work.

In late October the miners returned to work. The arbitrators awarded them a ten percent wage increase and a cut in working hours. Pennsylvania's workers inspired workers across the nation to ask for similar improvements. In 1916 the federal government passed the first child labor laws. A major labor reform bill, the Wagner Act, was passed in 1935. These changes improved conditions for workers all over Pennsylvania and the United States.

In the meantime, industry in Pennsylvania had peaked and was starting downhill. Coal was being replaced as a fuel by oil, and Pennsylvania coal mines began to shut down. The major users of steel—railroads—were running into competition from trucks and cars.

More hard times for the country and the state followed. During the Great Depression of the 1930s, many businesses across the country closed. People were out of work. By 1932 unemployment had grown to twenty-five percent. In 1936 floods washed over many parts of Pennsylvania. They killed more than a hundred people and caused more than $40 million worth of damage.

The national economy picked up during World War II. Manufacturing plants that had run at half speed in the 1930s now hummed with activity. Factories were converted to produce tanks and airplanes. But in Pennsylvania it was not a lasting change. By the 1950s the economy went back to a downward trend. All over Pennsylvania, mines closed.

Thousands of people were again out of work. Railroading again went into a decline, and thousands more people were out of work. Pennsylvania's iron, steel, and coal had helped make the United States a world economic leader. But for the majority of citizens in the state, industrial growth had been a mixed blessing.

In the 1960s the federal government funded a program

Out-of-work steelworkers from the Pittsburgh area picketed their own union's headquarters in 1964 to express their dissatisfaction with how the union handled their affairs.

to improve conditions in the Appalachian Mountains. This region stretches from Maine to Alabama. Pennsylvania is one of the thirteen states that make up this region. The government began hundreds of projects to help these poor and out-of-work families. In addition, Pennsylvania began urban renewal programs in both the 1950s and the 1960s to improve life in its cities. In 1971 a state income tax was passed to maintain programs that were meeting the needs of the people.

The nuclear accident at Three Mile Island had an enormous effect on the American nuclear power industry. The accident increased people's concern about the safety of nuclear power and caused the government to delay approving plans for new reactors during the 1980s.

Then, in 1972 a natural disaster occurred when a tropical storm hit the East Coast, causing 55 deaths. There was $3 billion worth of property damage in Pennsylvania. In 1979 another disaster struck. An accident at the Three Mile Island nuclear power plant near Harrisburg threatened to leak radiation into the area. Scientists and Three Mile Island employees succeeded in preventing a major catastrophe. But a small amount of radiation did leak out. Another disaster visited northern Pennsylvania in 1985. A group of tornadoes killed 65 people and injured about 700 more. The damage added up to more than $375 million.

Still, while all of this was going on, the farmers of Pennsylvania kept farming. The state remained a major power in national politics. It is still one of the most populated states, now ranked fifth in the country. It remains an industrial leader. William Penn could never have imagined the future of his woodland colony.

Society Hill

At one time, the older families of Philadelphia thought of themselves as the new American aristocracy. They saw their city as the center of culture in the New World. Their own neighborhood within Philadelphia was made up of families who controlled a great deal of wealth and power. Today, this historic area is called Society Hill.

The Biddle family has lived in Society Hill for many generations. Nicholas Biddle was president of the Bank of the United States, beginning in 1823. He was also a very important figure in Philadelphia's history. As his great-great grandson James said, "Nicholas Biddle was one man who really controlled the finances of the country. He was the artistic and social leader of the city. He presided over all this from this house." The house that James spoke of still stands on Society Hill.

Eventually, Philadelphia lost its position of power. It still had the powerful old families. It also had its history as the "City of Brotherly Love." It was the capital of the colonies and the United States from 1790 to 1800. But New York was becoming the center of finance, and the future seemed to lie in the West. According to James Biddle, "Philadelphia began to slip into its past. The stage of history had moved on from Philadelphia and left the town with its memories."

Philadelphians claim that Elfreth's Alley, part of Society Hill, is the oldest residential street in America.

Nicholas Biddle lost his post as bank president when political pressure caused President Andrew Jackson to close the bank in 1836.

And it has been mainly Society Hill, largely restored in the 1950s, that has kept these memories alive. The neighborhood has its share of modern structures. But much of it looks just as it did when Charles Biddle, the father of Nicholas, heard the Declaration of Independence for the first time. His diary entry for July 4, 1776, reads, "I walked to the statehouse to hear the Declaration read. No one of any importance was there." Little did he know these "unimportant" people would become our nation's leaders.

Johnstown's Roots Hold Fast

Johnstown has floods. Three times in just over the last hundred years, major floods have rushed through the streets, destroying everything in their way. And each time, the people of Johnstown have rebuilt their town.

Johnstown was named after its founder, a Swiss immigrant named Joseph Johns. It officially became a city in 1889. The city's worst—and most famous—flood hit in May that same year. During a torrential rainstorm, the South Fork Dam, which held a major reservoir, collapsed. A tremendous amount of water came gushing down the Conemaugh Valley, sweeping over Johnstown and everything else in its way. More than two thousand people were killed, and over $10 million in property was destroyed. But the city survived.

After a second flood killed 25 people in 1936, a flood control system was built. But in July 1977, the Conemaugh River overflowed anyway. That flood took another 85 lives and damaged more than $300 million in property.

So why do people still stay in Johnstown? "Our parents were primarily European immigrants," one resident explained, "and they muddled through a lot harder times than this. People put up with three floods. They came here, they live in a place like this where it's cold, but they seem to stay for some reason. Why? I don't know. Might be their roots."

The floodwaters of 1889 were powerful enough to uproot trees and overturn buildings.

Roots are what has kept one Johnstown family, the St. Clairs, in the city their ancestors chose. When times get tough, the St. Clair family takes care of its own. Several years ago, Bethlehem Steel started laying off workers. One of them was Tim Mihalic, who is married to Linda St. Clair.

"I'll do anything," Tim said. "Haul coal, cut grass, paint houses, build stuff. Anything. We manage. And [Linda's] father, . . . he's just like a second father. Whenever you need him, he's there."

The importance of family has been passed on to the younger generations of Johnstown. As Greg St. Clair, Linda's brother, said, "As far as college goes, it doesn't matter if I leave, but I'd like to come back to Johnstown. That's where my family is, and my family's a very important part of my life."

You may have heard people say "blood is thicker than water." It is an old saying that simply means that family relationships are stronger than any other relationship. Maybe this saying is a little more true in Johnstown than anywhere else.

Johnstown had made a remarkable recovery by 1940, only four years after the town's second disastrous flood in 1936.

Things Are Built to Last

Many facts about Pennsylvania seem to contradict each other. It is one of the nation's leading manufacturing states. But farmlands cover almost one third of the state. This gives Pennsylvania the largest rural population in the country, even though most of the people there live in cities. In addition, although Pennsylvania is a leader in manufacturing, about three quarters of the state's workers are employed in service industries. These are jobs in which people do work for or serve other people and don't manufacture anything at all. But such contradictions are part of what makes Pennsylvania flourish.

In the past the coal and steel industries overshadowed many others in Pennsylvania. Many people don't realize how important the service industry of retail sales has always been to this state. In fact, the nation's first department store opened in Philadelphia in the 1870s. And the first successful dime store, Woolworth's, started in Lancaster, Pennsylvania.

Although steel manufacturing played a large role in Pennsylvania's economy at one time, today the state's economy benefits from a wide range of products.

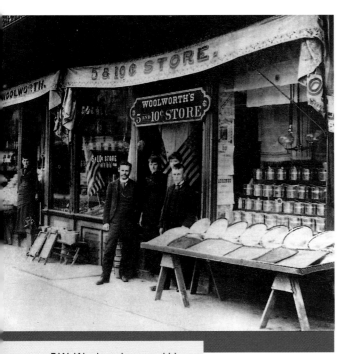

F.W. Woolworth opened his first store in Lancaster, Pennsylvania, in 1879. It was so successful that he established about twenty more of his dime stores during the next ten years in Pennsylvania and in surrounding states.

Today retail sales are the third most important service industry in Pennsylvania. Most important are social and personal services, such as hotels, hospitals, and law firms. Banks, insurance companies, and real estate companies are the second most important grouping of service industries. Other top areas include government, transportation, and communication.

About ten years ago, the manufacturing industry accounted for almost ninety percent of the state's income. Today, it makes up only twenty percent. Manufacturing is still important, however. An industry with a tradition that dates back to before the American Revolution doesn't easily disappear. Today the major manufacturing industries in Pennsylvania are metals, food products, chemicals, industrial machinery, printing and publishing, and electronics.

Steel and machinery manufacturing carried Pennsylvania's economy for most of its history. The state still leads the nation in production of specialty steel. But by the 1990s, food processing also became an important manufacturing industry in Pennsylvania. Factories here make beer, bread, cakes, cookies, crackers, and prepared meats. It is one of the nation's largest producers of snack foods and candy products. The world's largest chocolate and cocoa factory is in Hershey, Pennsylvania.

The chemical industry made a strong showing in the 1990s. Prescription drugs and medicine lead the chemical industry. In fact, the stretch of Route 202 just west of Philadelphia is called Medical Mile. The area is home to some of the country's largest drug companies, as well as research laboratories and medical schools.

Because there is so much manufacturing in Pennsylvania, agriculture and livestock account for only about one percent of the value of goods produced in the state. That one percent, however, is worth almost $3 billion. Pennsylvania has about 50,000 farms. Most of these are small, averaging about 150 acres. Nearly four million people live

above. Food processing is Pennsylvania's major manufacturing industry. The first commercial pretzel bakery in the United States opened near Lancaster in 1861.

below. The steel industry is no longer crucial to Pennsylvania's economy, but the state still leads the nation in the production of specialty steel.

Eastern Pennsylvania has the highest concentration of dairy farms in the state.

in the rural areas in Pennsylvania, keeping these farms going.

Most of Pennsylvania's farm income—about seventy percent—is from livestock and livestock products. Milk is the biggest farm product in Pennsylvania. The state is also a leader in eggs and poultry. Cattle raised for beef are another leading farm product.

The other thirty percent of the state's farm income comes from crops. The variety of crops grown in Pennsylvania is pretty amazing. The state leads the nation in mushrooms. Its major fruit crops are peaches and apples, but it also grows a lot of cherries, grapes, and strawberries. Other important crops include corn, hay, and potatoes. Much of the corn and hay produced goes to the state's livestock farmers, who use it to feed their beef and dairy cattle.

The lumber industry has become very important to Pennsylvania's economy in recent years. The state exports many millions of board feet of hardwoods to Canada, Japan, and Europe every year. The quality of Pennsylvania's cherry, oak, and maple lumber is known throughout the world.

Pennsylvania has another unusual quality, which helps in all its areas of work. A large part of the farms in the state have been owned by the same families on the same land for over one hundred years. The same kind of stability can be found in Pennsylvania's cities, also. People tend to stay in the same neighborhood. That's probably the best reason of all why things in Pennsylvania are built to last.

The Pennsylvania farms that help support the state's economy also provide beautiful land-scapes.

Chocolate Town, U.S.A.

Imagine a town with 23 acres of gardens and a zoo with 75 species of animals. Add to that an amusement park, museum, and theater. The air is filled with the smell of chocolate. Could such a place be real? One man's hard work and vision built this dream town into a reality. If you travel to

Whimsical **Hershey's Kiss** *streetlamps amuse tourists who visit Hershey, Pennsylvania.*

Milton S. Hershey played a key role in popularizing milk chocolate candy in countries all over the world.

Hershey, Pennsylvania, you will see it for yourself.

Milton S. Hershey began his career as a candy maker at the age of sixteen. But he did not become successful until he was nearly forty. Then he founded the Lancaster Caramel Company in Lancaster, Pennsylvania. The caramels became very popular, and Milton Hershey became very rich.

In 1900 Mr. Hershey sold his caramel company. He believed that making milk chocolate candy would lead to even greater success. He decided to build a chocolate factory.

He needed a location near plenty of fresh milk and a good supply of water. He needed hardworking people to help make the candy. He decided the perfect place was Derry, Pennsylvania, where he had been born. His wife and friends thought his idea was foolish. Why build the factory out in the cornfields and dairy pastures of rural Pennsylvania? But Milton Hershey had an idea.

He wasn't going to build just a factory. He was going to build a wonderful town with the factory in it. Starting in 1903, Hershey built his factory along with a bank and a park. He built a zoo, a department store, churches, and a school. He even built a trolley system to bring the workers in from nearby towns.

By 1910 Hershey chocolate was selling well, the chocolate factory was thriving, and so was the town of Hershey. But did Milton Hershey stop there? No. During the Great Depression of the 1930s, he kept people working. He had them build a sports arena and a community center. They also built a hotel and a theater. And they expanded the factory.

Milton Hershey died in 1945 at the age of 88. But his goals live on. Today, Hershey Chocolate U.S.A. is the world's largest chocolate manufacturing plant. They make 33 million *Hershey's Kisses* a day. The town has golf courses, a hockey team, and a symphony orchestra. The *HERSHEYPARK* amusement park covers 110 acres and has over 50 rides and attractions. More than two million people come every year to visit the little town that Milton Hershey built.

By the 1920s Hershey chocolate products were well established, and the factory provided a variety of jobs for area residents.

33

A Keystone of Inspiration

Pennsylvania has been producing writers and artists for almost as long as it has been producing coal and lawmakers. Some of the very first writers in the new country of the United States were natives of Pennsylvania. Charles Brockden Brown, author of the important early novel *Wieland*, was born in Philadelphia. A number of years later, a young author from Germantown started writing adventure stories for cheap magazines and went on to create a classic. Her name was Louisa May Alcott, and her book *Little Women* gave us a whole family full of bright, interesting girls, who have inspired generations of young women.

Pennsylvania has also produced plenty of poets. Poet, novelist, and critic Gertrude Stein began writing in Pennsylvania before moving to Paris. Pulitzer Prize winner Stephen Vincent Benét was born in Bethlehem. Wallace Stevens, one of the most important modern American poets, was born in Reading.

The Pennsylvania Dutch are descendants of German settlers who emigrated in the late 1600s. They are well-known for their distinctive folk art.

In addition to being a successful author, Louisa May Alcott was a promoter of women's rights and social reform.

And Hilda Doolittle, a poet better known as H.D., was another Bethlehem native.

In the second half of the nineteenth century, Pennsylvania actor Joseph Jefferson toured the United States enchanting audiences in small mining towns in Colorado and in large cities such as San Francisco and New York City. Pennsylvania has since kept this tradition of fine actors. Pennsylvanians of the silver screen include W. C. Fields, Jimmy Stewart, and Bill Cosby. And a television entertainer you may have heard of, Dick Clark, got his start in Philadelphia. His famous show *American Bandstand* started there in 1957.

Pennsylvania isn't any less important when it comes to artists. Many art historians believe that American painting was forever changed in the early twentieth century by Thomas Eakins. He was a painter and instructor at the Pennsylvania Academy of the Fine Arts, which still turns out artists today. Many other influential artists got their start in Pennsylvania. Mary Cassatt was one of the few female painters of a style called *impressionism*. And the mobile was invented by sculptor Alexander Calder, another Pennsylvania native. Artist Andy Warhol's famous paintings of Campbell's soup cans were first displayed at Philadelphia's Institute of Contemporary Art in 1964. Warhol had to be lifted through a skylight to escape the huge crowd of people that came to his opening night!

Few states can equal the cultural heritage found in Pennsylvania. Its writers and artists have come not just out of the major cities, but also out of the coal-mining towns, the steel-making towns, and the rolling green countryside. They have had the cultural advantages of many years of support for the arts. They have had the muscle and bone of hardworking families in hardworking towns. And today Pennsylvania's 38 professional dance companies, 41 orchestras, and scores of musicians, theaters, and performing arts centers help keep the state's cultural tradition alive.

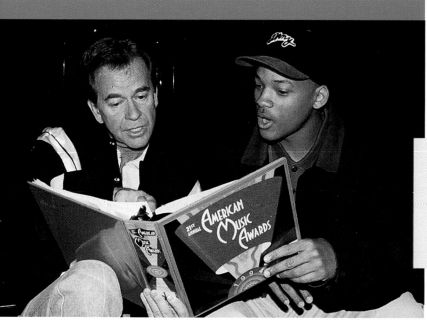

Dick Clark's youthful appearance has earned him the title "the world's oldest teenager." Both Dick Clark and Will Smith started their careers in Philadelphia.

A Glorious Voice

Marian Anderson loved to sing. She sang in the school choir as a child and in the Philadelphia Choral Society when she was a young woman. After her first performance at the Metropolitan Opera, her love of singing was met by the loving appreciation of every member of the audience.

Marian Anderson was born in 1902, the oldest of three daughters. Her father died when Marian was young. Her mother supported the family by working as a cleaner in a department store. Although there was very little money in the family, there was a great deal of love. When Marian Anderson was paid five dollars for singing, she gave a dollar each to her two sisters and two dollars to her mother. The dollar she kept paid for her own transportation to her next singing job.

However, Marian Anderson faced something less than love many times. As a teenager she was denied admission to a Philadelphia music school. They told her, "We don't take Colored." She was forced to ride in the "Jim Crow" cars of the train on her way to sing in her first concert

The same year Marian Anderson first performed at the Lincoln Memorial, the National Association for the Advancement of Colored People awarded her the Spingarn Medal for her outstanding contribution to her field.

Marian Anderson returned to the Lincoln Memorial in 1952 to sing at the funeral service of Harold Ickes, who had arranged her 1939 performance at the Memorial.

invited to Constitution Hall in Washington, D.C., but a group called the Daughters of the American Revolution barred her from making an appearance because of her race. Eleanor Roosevelt, the wife of the President of the United States, was a member of the Daughters of the American Revolution at that time. But when Mrs. Roosevelt heard what the group had done, she resigned in protest. She arranged for Marian Anderson to sing at the Lincoln Memorial instead. More than 75,000 people of all races came to the concert on that Easter Sunday.

Marian Anderson was the first African American member of the Metropolitan Opera. In her autobiography *My Lord, What a Morning* she described the experience. "I will never forget the wholehearted responsiveness of the public. I may have dreamed of such things, but I had not foreseen that I would play a part in the reality."

Throughout her career Marian Anderson encouraged other African Americans to "realize that the doors everywhere may open increasingly to those who have prepared themselves well. . . ."

in Washington, D.C. Those were the only train cars African Americans were allowed to ride as passengers.

Despite these problems, she continued to sing. Soon she established herself as a top American concert performer. In 1939 she was

Shifting Resources to Meet the Future

Pennsylvania grew rapidly when it started over three hundred years ago. Then, in this century, the state went through some very difficult times. Industry was its backbone, and industry changed. But Pennsylvania has always looked toward the future. The state has been one of the nation's leaders in research and invention ever since George Washington granted the first patent to Philadelphian Samuel Hopkins in 1790. After all, it was the University of Pennsylvania where the first electronic computer was run, in 1946. And today, Pennsylvania ranks fourth in the country in the number of research centers. As if that's not enough to keep the state ahead in technology, it has one of the largest numbers of high-technology workers in the country.

Technological advances aside, it is the state's people who have kept Pennsylvania's hope for the future alive. From the time of William Penn, this has been a state based on tolerance. Different people with different religious and ethnic backgrounds came and

Despite a decline in steel manufacturing in the 1970s and 1980s, Pittsburgh continues to prosper from other industries such as glass, petroleum, electrical equipment, and chemical products.

The University of Pennsylvania was instrumental in the technology revolution. Their ENIAC (Electronic Numerical Integrator and Calculator) computer (built in 1946) was the first all-electronic computer.

were accepted. You didn't have to be like everyone else to be welcome in Pennsylvania. You didn't have to change your ways once you arrived here. So today you'll find a strong Italian community next door to a strong Polish community. You'll find the Amish and the Mennonites living quietly among their more

Pennsylvania has one of the largest Amish communities in the United States. The Amish are a religious farming group that hold to a simple way of life.

modern neighbors. These strong communities have given Pennsylvania stability. People tend to stay, to live, and to work in their communities.

Pennsylvania is within five hundred miles of nearly fifty percent of the United States population. That's a powerful position! Pennsylvania is so close to so many people because many of America's largest cities are located in the East. Having access to so many people has opened up many distribution and manufacturing centers in the state. Pennsylvania has looked ahead to build roads, airports, and railroads to encourage more manufacturing markets.

But a lot remains to be done to complete the transition from old to new. Too many people in the inner cities of Pennsylvania are still poor. As strong as the state is economically, there are too many people without jobs.

At the annual New Year's Day Mummers' Parade, musicians dress in elaborate costumes and march down Broad Street in Philadelphia.

Pennsylvanians live with the lesson of Three Mile Island, too. Their history reminds them that the industrial problems of the future could make those of the past seem small by comparison. One of the ways they are trying to prevent future environmental problems is through statewide recycling programs. Recent laws have made Pennsylvania the first large state to require recycling. Such efforts to help the environment have also created new jobs.

Although Pennsylvania's natural resources have dwindled, its human resources remain rich. That's the most important factor in a well-run state. These human resources are helping Pennsylvania move confidently into the future.

Although Philadelphia is one of the oldest cities in the United States, modern skyscrapers are the most noticeable feature of its present-day skyline.

Important Historical Events

1609 British explorer Henry Hudson sails into Delaware Bay.

1643 The Swedes build a fort on Tinicum Island, near present-day Philadelphia.

1655 Dutch troops under the command of Peter Stuyvesant come from New Netherland to capture New Sweden.

1664 The English take control of the Pennsylvania region.

1681 King Charles II grants Pennsylvania to William Penn in payment of a debt to Penn's father.

1683 Pennsylvania adopts William Penn's "Frame of Government."

1701 Penn writes a new constitution called the "Charter of Privileges."

1708 Iron ore is discovered in the Delaware Valley.

1740 The state university is founded in Philadelphia.

1753 The Liberty Bell is hung in the Pennsylvania State House in Philadelphia.

1754 The French and Indian War begins, and lasts until 1763.

1774 The First Continental Congress meets in Philadelphia.

1775 The Revolutionary War begins in April. The Second Continental Congress meets in Philadelphia in May.

1776 Congress adopts the Declaration of Independence at the State House.

1777 The British occupy Philadelphia. The Articles of Confederation are drawn up. Washington's troops camp at Valley Forge.

1778 The British leave Philadelphia, and the Congress returns.

1787 The Constitutional Convention meets in Philadelphia where the U.S. Constitution is drafted. Pennsylvania becomes the second state to ratify.

1790 The first stock exchange is begun in Philadelphia.

1811 Robert Fulton's steamboat *New Orleans* is launched from Pittsburgh.

1834 The Pennsylvania Canal System links Philadelphia and Pittsburgh.

1846 The Pennsylvania Railroad is chartered.

1859 Edwin Drake drills the first successful oil well near Titusville.

1863 Union troops defeat General Robert E. Lee at the Battle of Gettysburg. Lincoln delivers the Gettysburg Address.

1889 The first Johnstown flood kills more than 2,000 people.

1940 The Pennsylvania Turnpike opens and runs from Middlesex to Irwin.

1946 The first electronic computer is run at the University of Pennsylvania.

1971 Pennsylvania adopts an individual income tax to help increase revenues.

1979 An accident at Three Mile Island raises concerns about the safety of nuclear power plants.

1985 Tornadoes in northern Pennsylvania kill 65 people and injure 700 more.

1993 Vice President Al Gore dedicates the $522 million Pennsylvania Convention Center. It is the most expensive public works project in Philadelphia's history.

The flag features the state seal flanked on both sides by horses. The seal portrays a shield with a ship, a plow, and bundles of wheat. An olive branch adorns the right side of the shield, and a stalk of corn is on the left side. An eagle, the symbol of America, stands above.

Pennsylvania Almanac

Nickname. The Keystone State

Capital. Harrisburg

State Bird. Ruffed grouse

State Flower. Mountain laurel

State Tree. Hemlock

State Motto. Virtue, Liberty, and Independence

State Song. None

State Abbreviations. Pa. or Penn. (traditional); PA (postal)

Statehood. December 12, 1787, the 2nd state

Government. Congress: U.S. senators, 2; U.S. representatives, 21; State Legislature: senators, 50; representatives, 203; Counties: 67

Area. 45,308 sq mi (117, 348 sq km), 33rd in size among the states

Greatest Distances. north/south, 175 mi (282 km); east/west, 306 mi (493 km)

Elevation. Highest: Mount Davis, 3,213 ft (979 m). Lowest: sea level, along the Delaware River

Population. 1990 Census: 11,924,710 (0.5% increase over 1980), 5th among the states. Density: 263 persons per sq mi (102 persons per sq km). Distribution: 69% urban, 31% rural. 1980 Census: 11,864,751

Economy. *Agriculture:* milk, beef cattle, eggs, poultry, mushrooms, apples, peaches. *Manufacturing:* metals, industrial machinery, food processing, printing and publishing, chemicals, electric and electronic equipment. *Mining:* coal, limestone

State Seal

State Flower: Mountain laurel

State Bird: Ruffed grouse

Annual Events

★ Mummers Parade in Philadelphia (New Year's Day)

★ Ice Carving Festival in White Haven (January)

★ Groundhog Day in Punxsutawney (February)

★ Memorial Day Celebration in Gettysburg (last Monday in May)

★ All American Teddy Bears' Picnic in Lahaska (July)

★ Philadelphia Freedom Festival (July)

★ Little League Baseball World Series in South Williamsport (August)

★ Fall Foliage Festivals in all regions (October)

★ Reenactment of Washington Crossing the Delaware in Washington Crossing (Christmas Day)

Places to Visit

★ Allegheny National Forest

★ Chocolate World in Hershey

★ Drake Well Museum in Titusville

★ Eckley Miners Village in Hazelton

★ Elfreth's Alley and Independence Hall in Philadelphia

★ Frank Lloyd Wright's Fallingwater House and Museum in Mill Run

★ The Franklin Institute Science Museum in Philadelphia

★ Gettysburg National Military Park

★ Hawk Mountain Bird Sanctuary in the Kittatinny Mountains

★ Landis Valley Museum of the Pennsylvania Dutch in Lancaster

★ Longwood Gardens in Kennett Square

★ Railroad Museum of Pennsylvania in Strasburg

★ Valley Forge National Historical Park

Index